George Eastman

Photography Pioneer

Peter Brooke-Ball

**BLACKBIRCH™
PRESS**

San Diego • Detroit • New York • San Francisco • Cleveland
New Haven, Conn. • Waterville, Maine • London • Munich

Photo Credits: AP Photo: cover; The Advertising Archives: 34, 35 (top left); AKG: 28 (top),
Allsport UK Ltd: 20–21 (both)/John Gichigi, 58–59/Gray Mortimore; Ann Ronan: 18, 22
(both), 29 (top), 35 (top right and bottom), 38 (bottom); J.L. Charmet: 12; Edimedia: 28
(bottom)/Coll Kharbine; Gamma: 5/Ferry-Liaison, 30 (top), 32–33 (main pic)/Phil Matt, 55
(top)/Eric Bouvet, 59 (top)/G. Merillon, (bottom)/Gilles Saussier; George Eastman House:
42/Joseph Dinunzio; Image Select: 36 (bottom), 45, 47, 50–51 (all); The Kobal Collection:
46; Kodak Limited: 30 (bottom), 33 (inset, both), 54, 56 (all), 57, 60/Jim McGuckin; The
National Museum of Photography, Film and Television: 7 (top), 9 (bottom), 13, 25 (bottom), 27, 38 (top), 48 (bottom); NMPFT/Science and Society Picture Library: 10;
Popperfoto: 26; Range/Bettmann: 9 (top), 48 (top), 49, Rex Features: 4/Henryk T. Kaiser,
19, 44; Royal Photographic Society: 6/Cuthbert Bede, 7 (bottom)/L. Tisserand, 11, 15, 23,
24, 29 (bottom), 31, 36 (top), 37 (bottom), 39, 40 (all), Baron De Meyer (bottom right
only); The Science Museum: 8, 25 (top), 37 (top).

LIBRARY OF CONGRESS CATALOGING-IN-PUBLICATION DATA

Brooke-Ball, Peter.
  George Eastman / by Peter Brooke-Ball.
    p. cm. — (Giants of American industry)
Summary: A brief biography of George Eastman, who simplified the complicated
process of photography so that he was able "to make the camera as convenient
as the pencil."
Includes bibliographical references and index.
  ISBN 1-4103-0070-6 (hardback : perm. paper)
  1. Eastman, George, 1854–1932—Juvenile literature. 2. Photographic industry—
United States—Biography—Juvenile literature. [1. Eastman, George, 1854–1932. 2.
Inventors. 3. Photography—History.] I. Title. II. Series.

TR140.E3B75 2004
770'.92—dc21
                                                          2003005142

Contents

"As convenient as the pencil"

Kodak is one of the most famous brand names in the world. To most people, regardless of the language they speak, it represents just one thing—photography. The man who created the company and simplified the complicated process of photography was George Eastman.

George Eastman took up photography as a hobby when he was twenty-four. At that time, it was a relatively new art form enjoyed only by an elite group of people. He quickly spotted its potential and resolved "to make the camera as convenient as the pencil."

Eastman had discovered a hobby that was ripe for development, and with his tirelessly inventive mind and his acute business sense, he succeeded where others with similar ambitions had failed. Within the span of just twenty years, he and his company made photography available to millions.

Opposite: Kodak introduced the world's first slide film in 1935. Above: Kodak cameras can be used in all situations, even in war zones.

• • • • • • • • • • • • • • • • • •

"Kodak's aim is to be the best in the world at what we do— to set the standards that others have to follow."

—**From** *Kodak in the U.K.,* **a Kodak publication**

• • • • • • • • • • • • • • • • • •

As his company grew, Eastman became wealthy and powerful. He was shrewd in business, but he was never a conventional businessman. He shunned personal publicity. He looked after his employees as if they were members of his extended family. He also gave away the bulk of his fortune.

By the 1990s, Eastman's Kodak Company had become one of the twenty-five largest businesses in the United States. Its interests and influence had spread far beyond the confines of photography. Kodak also manufactured pharmaceuticals, textiles, and electronic goods. It had come a long way from its modest start in a rented warehouse attic.

A hobby

After he had worked for four solid years as a bank clerk, twenty-four-year-old George Eastman decided that he deserved a break. He wanted to move somewhere as different as possible from Rochester, New York, his hometown on the southern shore of Lake Ontario. The city of Santo Domingo, on the Caribbean island of Hispaniola, seemed to be just the right place.

Getting to Hispaniola, however, posed a few problems. The year was 1878. Long-distance travel was expensive, slow, and potentially dangerous. These factors were not enough to prevent George Eastman from planning his long-awaited trip, however.

A friend suggested that he take a camera with him on the trip. The friend thought that if any of the pictures were good, Eastman might be able to sell them when he got back. Eastman knew that this would be an amazing experience, and that his friend was right. The journey would be worth recording. He spent a whole month's salary on a photographic kit. Little did he know where that one purchase would lead him.

A change of heart

Eastman described the photographic kit as "a packhorse load" of equipment—and his kit contained only the basic essentials. It included a black developing tent, developing trays, assorted bottles of

This drawing points out how heavy and awkward photographic equipment used to be. George Eastman, founder of the Kodak company, was determined to change that.

PHOTOGRAPHIC PLEASURES

POPULARLY PORTRAYED WITH PEN & PENCIL,
BY CUTHBERT BEDE, B.A.
AUTHOR OF "VERDANT GREEN."

"START INTO LIGHT, AND MAKE THE LIGHTER START!"
REJECTED ADDRESSES.

Above: In the mid-1800s, some photographers sold their services from horse-drawn carriages.

Left: In this drawing, a photographer readies the camera as his assistant stands by with a prepared wet plate. Eastman perfected the use of the dry plate.

chemicals, and large jugs for water. The camera itself was a large wooden box.

This, however, was by no means all the equipment a photographer of the time needed. A photographer also needed a sturdy tripod to hold the camera perfectly still for the ten to forty seconds that it took to take a picture. In addition, the photographic images were made on heavy, fragile glass plates inserted into the back of the camera. These plates had to be coated with photographic emulsion just before each picture was taken. This emulsion was wet, so the process was called "wet-plate" photography. All the preparation of the plates and subsequent developing had to be carried out quickly and in total darkness. Overall, it took more than twenty minutes to take just one photograph.

Despite all the cumbersome gear and the disappointments of the unreliable techniques that were standard at the time, Eastman found himself increasingly absorbed by the process of photography. The more photographs he took, the more he wanted to learn. Slowly, the pull of Hispaniola gave way to the even greater lure of the camera, and he put off the trip. He remembered, though, "That did not matter so much because, in making ready, I had become wholly absorbed by photography."

Eastman became quite an expert at taking photographs, even though he insisted that he was an amateur. He wanted the word amateur to be interpreted literally as "one who carries out his art for the love of it." Eastman loved all the chemical processes involved in photography and had the persistence of a true inventor.

Inventor

Although George Eastman was captivated by photography, he gradually became more frustrated by it. The procedures were complicated and difficult to carry out, and there was so much that could go wrong at each stage. He decided to look for ways to simplify the steps. He started with the messy and precarious business of preparing the photographic plates. Although he had no training in chemistry, George Eastman pored over journals and books, looking for possible changes to this process. He even taught himself basic French and German so that he could read international photography magazines.

One evening, as he flipped through a British photography article, he recognized a solution to his problem. A few dedicated photographers in the United Kingdom were experimenting with different kinds of emulsions. Plates coated with these new homemade emulsions remained sensitive to light for months after they were dry. This meant that wet plates could be things of the past. Too impatient to wait for others to perfect the new emulsions, Eastman began to concoct his own versions in his mother's kitchen.

Inventor turned entrepreneur

It did not take Eastman long to realize that if he could perfect the recipe, he could make photographic

This camera was used by the French painter Louis Daguerre, after whom the daguerreotype photograph was named.

Opposite: This 1884 picture of Eastman was one of the first photographs to be taken on American film, one of his many photographic inventions.

Above: George was the youngest child in his family.

plates, not only for himself, but for others as well. He could go into business. With fiery determination, George Eastman worked in the bank during the day and turned his mother's kitchen into an improvised laboratory at night He frequently became so worn out with his experiments that he fell asleep, fully clothed, beside the kitchen stove.

Eastman was a perfectionist and was not dismayed by his frequent failures. If anything, they spurred him on. Gradually, he moved closer to his goal. It took him two years to formulate an emulsion recipe with which he was truly happy. He was then twenty-six, and his emulsion became the foundation of one of the most powerful and influential companies in the world, the Eastman Kodak Company.

A tough beginning

George Eastman was born on July 12, 1854, to relatively wealthy parents, George Washington and Maria Kilbourn Eastman. His father ran a nursery business in the small upstate New York town of Waterville and earned more than enough money to support his wife and three children—George and his two elder sisters, Ellen and Emma.

George Sr. was ambitious. When his son was six, he moved the family to the flourishing town of Rochester to establish a business school called the Eastman Commercial College. At first, the college was a success. Just two years after the family arrived in Rochester, however, George Sr. died suddenly. Without its founder, the college began to fail. In a short time, the once-prosperous Eastman family was left almost penniless.

Maria Eastman was very resourceful, however, and she used her one remaining asset, the family home, to make money. She began to take in lodgers. By saving what little she had, Maria managed to keep her family together.

Young George's school career was unremarkable. He was meticulous in his work but was not academically brilliant. He preferred to play baseball and have fun.

George left school when he was just fourteen. One of his sisters contracted polio and became disabled. Shouldering responsibility for the family, George took a job as an insurance messenger boy. At age fifteen, he moved to another insurance company and worked his way up to become a filing clerk with a salary of five dollars a week. George knew, however, that five dollars a week would never be enough to provide adequately for his family, and he could see that he needed specialized skills and experience to get a better job. So, he started to study accounting in the evenings. Then, in 1874, at the age of twenty, he got a job as a junior clerk at the Rochester Savings Bank.

George Eastman was dedicated to his job at the bank. He was driven and motivated, and he worked hard. Eastman used the money he made to support his mother and sisters. He also saved a few cents out of each paycheck for himself. By the time he began planning his trip to Hispaniola in 1878, he had saved $3,000.

The first photographers

When Eastman first stumbled into photography that same year, the discipline was still very much in its infancy. It had not advanced very much since its invention in 1826 when a French chemist named Joseph Niepce took the first photograph, a faint image on a metal plate. Niepce teamed up with another Frenchman, painter Louis Daguerre, and together they perfected what became known as the daguerreotype, a kind of photograph made on copper sheets coated with iodized silver. The first daguerreotype was made in 1839. In the same year, an Englishman named William Fox Talbot made what he called a "photographic drawing" on silver chloride paper. Two years later, Talbot invented the first negative from which prints could be made.

At that time, photography was largely in the hands of those who were wealthy enough to finance their own experiments. Progress was slow, and the next step forward did not come until 1851, when

This portrait is a daguerreotype photograph, a method of photography created in 1839 by two Frenchmen.

Englishman William Fox Talbot experimented with this camera in 1839. His first photographic drawing, an image of a lattice window, is in the background.

Englishman Frederick Scott Archer invented the wet-plate process with which George Eastman became familiar. Cumbersome though it was, wet-plate photography was relatively reliable, and it enabled photographers to predict results with some degree of accuracy.

In 1871, some seven years before George Eastman became interested in taking pictures, a man named R.L. Maddox invented dry-plate photography. This type of photography did not become popular right away. Many photographers were not convinced that it had any future because the majority of pictures came out completely black. Others felt that the wet-plate system was adequate. As a result, dry-plate photography was largely ignored, and only a few photographers were willing to gamble with the new process. George Eastman was one of the few.

The value of patents

When Eastman finally put together a satisfactory emulsion recipe for dry-plate photography, he decid-

"George Eastman's inventive genius revolutionized photography. When he began as an amateur to take pictures, the technique of photography was difficult and the apparatus cumbersome. He made photographers of the world's people by simplifying the entire process."

—From *George Eastman*, a Kodak publication

ed to go into business selling dry plates. He acknowledged, though, that there was more to a successful business than a good idea and recognized that he had many challenges to overcome.

One problem the twenty-six-year-old had to address was the way in which he coated the plates with the emulsion. So far, he had simply brushed it on by hand. This, however, was a slow process that would be impossible to sustain if his business were to grow and succeed. To overcome this problem, Eastman constructed a machine to coat the plates. Mass production of uniform and reliable products was, he believed, the key to success in business.

Eastman recognized the value of his machine and decided to patent its design. In this way, he became the only person with the right to make and sell the machine. Anyone who wanted to copy or use it had to pay him a fee. Patents have to be taken out separately in individual countries, however, and since England was the place where most advances in photography were being made, Eastman decided to patent his machine there first. In 1879, he took some money out of his savings account and traveled to England to obtain a British patent. When he returned to the United States, Eastman also took out a U.S. patent for the dry-plate coating machine.

His foresight was perfect. In October 1879, a British photography company called Mawson & Swan bought the right to manufacture and use George Eastman's dry-plate coating machine.

Open for business

Another problem that worried Eastman was how to finance his business. Although he had almost $3,000 saved, he needed more than that to establish a business. He had to buy equipment and materials, rent factory space, and pay workers' wages before he could expect any returns on sales. He wrote to his uncle Horace to ask for a loan. The conservative Horace thought the venture was far too risky, however, and rejected his nephew's plea for support.

Disappointed by his uncle's refusal to help,

Eastman decided to go into business anyway. He financed the venture with his savings and the money he had made from Mawson & Swan. In 1880, Eastman started to produce photographic dry plates from a rented attic in Rochester, New York.

To his surprise and relief, financial help soon arrived, although it was from an unexpected source. One of his mother's former lodgers, Henry Strong, was a successful manufacturer of whips for horse-drawn buggies, the most common transportation of the day. Strong knew little about photography, but he, like Eastman, was a shrewd businessman. He decided to invest in George Eastman's budding company, the Eastman Dry Plate Company. Eastman used Strong's money to buy equipment, pay his one employee, and rent a new building. In exchange, Strong expected to take a share of the company's profits. If the business failed, however, Strong stood to lose his money.

Strong also became a partner and joint owner of the company. As partners, Eastman and Strong were responsible for the company's operations and business decisions. As in all successful partnerships, the two men trusted each other. Eastman valued Strong's understanding of business issues, and Strong believed in Eastman's ambitions and his knowledge of photography.

Eastman's dry plates were first manufactured commercially in 1880.

Faulty products

When the Eastman Dry Plate Company moved to the third floor of a warehouse in Rochester, twenty-seven-year-old Eastman still worked at the bank during the day. He prepared emulsions during the evening and had only one assistant to help him run the business.

That soon changed as sales began to pick up, though. There were still relatively few people who took photographs, but those who did were enthusi-

"My desires are only limited by my imagination."

—George Eastman, 1896

15

While in his thirties, Eastman posed for this formal portrait.

astic. They frequently discussed new photographic inventions. Their opinions of Eastman's dry plates were good. Both amateurs and professionals praised the plates' quality. The *Philadelphia Photographer* magazine said, "The plates . . . negatives of both summer and winter scenes were characterized by a great delicacy of detail in either light or shadows. This I considered a most difficult test."

The increase in sales was so great that after just one year, the Eastman Dry Plate Company had moved to yet another larger facility. Eastman continued to work by day at the bank until September 1881. By then, the company was seeing profits of four thousand dollars a month.

The Eastman Dry Plate Company ran smoothly until 1882. Then, suddenly, people began to return the plates and complain that they were useless. When he examined the plates, Eastman had to agree, and he immediately searched for the cause of the problem. By March 1882, he had completed five hundred experiments but had been unable to identify the problem. After a hasty trip to Mawson & Swan in England, Eastman discovered that fault lay not in the photographic emulsion itself, but in impurities in the gelatin he had used to make it.

At considerable cost, Eastman replaced all the defective plates with new ones. "Making good on those plates took our last dollar," George Eastman recalled. "But what we had left was more important— reputation." To Eastman, replacing the faulty plates was the only thing to do, and that simple gesture did much to boost the reputation of the company.

By the end of 1882, the Eastman Dry Plate Company had made a considerable profit. Eastman decided to build a new factory, and he still had money left over, even after all expenses and wages had been paid. It was a formidable achievement to make such a profit after a year in which the company had been on the brink of collapse.

Marketing photography

In 1883, Eastman and Strong moved their company to another new and bigger factory. The growth of the company had been extraordinary, and its success was based on the creation of a new product of consistent quality and on the company's good reputation. These were two principles that encouraged photographers to buy Eastman's products over anyone else's.

The number of people interested in Eastman's product remained small, however. Few people had the means or equipment to take photographs. In addition, the art of photography was a complicated business, and most people were wary of it.

The photographic suppliers in the United States seemed happy with this situation. They marketed a limited number of products to established photographers and did not seem interested in branching out into the larger population. The ambitious Eastman, however, wanted to see his business grow. To him, ignoring the mainstream seemed like a waste of busi-

. . . .

"The ideal large corporation is the one that makes the best use of the brains within it."

—George Eastman

. . . .

ness potential. Thus, he investigated ways of making photography less exclusive.

To accomplish this, Eastman drafted four simple business guidelines that he believed were crucial for success. He wanted to mass-produce goods using machines, distribute goods nationally and internationally, advertise and sell products by demonstration, and keep prices low. To Eastman, these four ideas were inextricably linked. If a product were mass-produced, for example, it could be sold cheaply. In order to sell it, though, people had to be made aware of it through advertisements. Eastman also felt that there was little reason to limit himself to the U.S. market. He decided to export his products as well. In order to make this business plan work, though, Eastman first had to persuade people that photography was not as difficult as it seemed. He also needed to create and sell a product many people wanted to buy.

A name change

To make photography universally popular, Eastman knew that photographic equipment had to be simplified. The average person did not want to handle glass plates, heavy cameras, and all the other necessary equipment. He decided that the first place to make a change was to eliminate the glass plates themselves.

Eastman hypothesized that paper, instead of heavy glass plates, could be an effective support for a photographic emulsion. In many ways, paper was ideal. It was inexpensive. It was flexible, and it weighed very little. So, Eastman began to experiment once more and made an emulsion that could satisfactorily be mounted on very thin pieces of paper.

As he worked, he ran into a problem. Paper did not let light through. Any print made from a paper-based negative was always blurry. To make the paper transparent, Eastman formulated a special castor oil–based liquid called Translucene and brushed it onto the paper. The new product had only limited success, but Eastman thought it was

Opposite: This late-19th-century drawing shows a photographer operating a camera that used wet plates.

Below: Portrait photographers had to watch the time as they held a camera shutter open.

Modern technology allows rolls of exposed film to be developed in machines.

worth marketing. In 1884, he placed advertisements in leading photography magazines to promote the new product. They read, "Shortly after January 1, 1885, the Eastman Dry Plate and Film Company will introduce a new sensitive film which it is believed will prove an economical and convenient substitute for glass dry plates both for outdoor and studio work."

Eastman had changed his company's name because he believed strongly in the future of paper-based film. In addition, the new name accompanied changes in the company's makeup. It was no longer a simple part-nership between Eastman and Strong. The company now had fourteen other investors who stood to lose or gain money, depending on how it did. Henry Strong became the company's president, although he actually had little to do with day-to-day business. Eastman became treasurer and general manager. As treasurer, Eastman's task was to monitor the financial state of the company, and as general manager, it was his job to run the organization.

Room for improvement

Eastman's new film, which was manufactured in long strips, came with a special holder. This holder enabled a roll of paper negatives to be wound from one spool onto another. It had been devised by Eastman and a camera maker named William Walker.

The film came in a variety of sizes to suit different cameras and was specifically designed to replace tra-ditional glass plates. Each roll of film contained up to twenty-four exposures. This meant that a photogra-pher no longer had to carry a box of twenty-four heavy glass plates.

The roller and the paper film were revolutionary in their design. Not everybody saw them as such, though, and few people wanted to buy them. Eastman remembered, "When we started with our scheme of film photography we expected that everybody who used glass plates would take up films, but we found that the number who did so was relatively small and in order to make a large business we would have to reach the general public." Most photographers preferred to stick with the dry plates because they produced excellent quality prints, and the general public was still reluctant to take up photography as a hobby. As a result, paper film did not catch on.

Try again

Eastman was not deterred, however. By the end of 1885, he had begun to manufacture what he called American film. This had three layers: a paper support, a layer of water-soluble gelatin, and a top layer of photographic emulsion. After the film had been exposed, the photographer poured water over the top to melt the middle layer. The photographic emulsion was then stripped off and strengthened with a coating of another layer of gelatin. This strip was then dried and could be used to make prints. Before he marketed the American film, Eastman took the precaution of taking out patents not only on the product, but on the preparation processes as well.

The quality of American film negatives was excellent, but the developing process was very complicated. Although the product sold reasonably well, it failed to secure for Eastman the huge new market he was after.

Changing the paper

Always anxious to learn and to find ways to improve his product, George Eastman decided to use a different type of paper for photographic prints. He adapted his factory's filmmaking equipment to use bromide paper. Bromide had been largely ignored because it was messy and awkward and because negatives could be developed onto to it only in a darkroom. Silver chloride paper, which was clamped tightly to a negative and left in the sun until a positive image appeared, was often used instead.

Eastman, however, saw great potential in bromide paper. In particular, it could be used to make enlargements. In an effort to capitalize on this possibility,

Once developed and dry, negative film is used to create positive prints. Then, the film is cut and mounted in cardboard cases.

William Fox Talbot was the first to invent the negative (bottom)—from which multiple positive prints (top) can be made.

Eastman started to offer an enlargement service. For a fee, photographers could send negatives to his company and have prints made that were as large as thirty-by-twenty-five inches. This broke new ground. Until Eastman established this service, photographers had done their own developing and printing.

It was during 1886 that Eastman realized that his paper film was not going to revolutionize photography after all. He also began to accept his own limitations as a chemist. He had not been trained in chemistry, and he was merely a self-taught, although extremely successful, amateur. The development of the product he craved was beyond his skills, so he hired a research chemist named Henry Reichenbach. The newcomer was immediately given two tasks. First, he was to improve photographic emulsions so that they became faster and more sensitive. His second task was to create a strong, flexible, transparent film base on which those emulsions could be coated.

The "detective" camera

In the spring of 1887, Eastman turned his attention to manufacturing cameras. The first cameras produced by his company were simple dry-plate cameras, but he was really interested in the development of a successful "detective" camera. These cameras were so called because they were tiny in comparison with the bulky, large-format cameras that most photographers used. Eastman reasoned that the average person would be more attracted to a small camera than a big one. He also wanted to make a camera that used film and was, therefore, easy to operate.

Unfortunately for Eastman, the product was a dismal failure. His company produced only fifty, and few of those were actually sold. Although he was bitterly disappointed, Eastman refused to give up. He remained convinced that his basic idea of a compact, simple camera was a good one.

The birth of Kodak

A new word came into being in June 1888. At first, it left people puzzled. Some thought it came from an obscure foreign language. Others thought it was a meaningless joke. Before long, however, the word became common throughout the world and everyone knew what it meant. George Eastman invented the word *Kodak* to describe a new compact camera he had designed. For some time, he had searched for a strong, catchy name for the camera. Eastman explained how he came up with the name. "I devised the name myself. The letter 'K' had been a favorite with me—it seems a strong, incisive sort of letter. It became a question of trying out a great number of combinations of letters that made words starting and ending with a 'K'."

Eastman was quick to register the new word as a trademark. He knew he had created the perfect name for his new product. In Eastman's application for the trademark, he wrote, "Kodak—This is not a foreign name or word; it was constructed by me to serve a definite purpose. It has the following merits as a trademark word. First: It is short. Second: It is not

In 1888, Eastman marketed a simple, reliable camera—the original Kodak.

capable of mispronunciation. Third: It does not re-semble anything in the art and cannot be associated with anything in the art except the Kodak."

Opposite: Eastman knew the power of advertising. The Kodak Girl pictured in these posters from the early 1900s was recognized internationally.

Below: This 1895 badge advertised the simplicity of the Kodak.

The Kodak camera was light, compact, and easy to use. It did not even have a viewfinder, the device on a camera that shows what will be included in a picture. To take pictures with the Kodak camera, a photographer only had to aim a "V" embossed on the top of the casing at the subject. The camera also came loaded with enough film to take one hundred photographs. The photographer simply pulled a cord to prepare the shutter, wound the film, and pressed the button. George Eastman had successfully reduced the complicated process of photography to just three steps.

Careful expansion

The Kodak camera was successful for more than its design, however. For one, purchasers received more than just the camera itself. They also got a small notebook to record the details of each picture taken and an explanatory booklet called the *Kodak Primer* that was written by Eastman himself. In addition, because Eastman knew that most people were intimidated by photography and by the messy chemicals associated with it, he decided that his company should do all the developing. When photographers had used up their film, they sent the camera back to Eastman's factory. There, for a small fee, the film was developed and printed, and the camera loaded with fresh film.

Advertising also proved beneficial. Eastman came up with a unique but simple slogan to market the camera. It was, "You press the button—We do the rest." Then, determined to capture the interest of average people who had never taken a photograph before, Eastman advertised the camera in the popular press. Similarly, the camera could be bought from pharmacies and general stores, not just from photography stores.

Advertising

Eastman quickly became aware of the power of advertising. Promoting products was not a new idea, but Eastman was one of the first entrepreneurs to analyze it and to set aside a fixed amount of money to pay for advertisements.

One of his early marketing tools was the "Kodak Girl." This image of a beautiful and smiling woman quickly became something of an icon. She was always happy and surrounded by friends, and she always carried a Kodak camera. As Eastman intended, she particularly appealed to teenagers, the very people he wanted to convince to buy his products. The Kodak girl and her air of youthful freedom appeared in magazines, in newspapers, and on billboards. She also became known internationally; in Great Britain, she was dubbed the "Blue Girl," and in France, "Dame Kodak." In various guises, the Kodak Girl was used to promote Kodak products for decades. Eastman believed that to reinforce the name of Kodak, a consistently recognizable image was essential.

Eastman did not stick with just one idea to sell his cameras and film, however. He consistently sought out innovative techniques. One of his most successful ploys was to publish testimonials from famous people. He particularly liked what explorers had to say about his film and cameras, and he was delighted when the first man to reach the North Pole, Robert Peary, preferred Kodak products. Eastman also used one of the first electric billboards in London, England. He wooed the public with a huge electric billboard that flashed the single word *Kodak*. There was no need to explain who or what Kodak was. Everyone already knew.

Success

The Kodak camera became such a success that the word *Kodak* became synonymous with "camera"; people often said "Bring your Kodak" instead of "Bring your camera." Likewise, Eastman's advertising slogan entered the common language. Politicians and comedians often incorporated "You press the button— We do the rest" into speeches and performances.

In 1888, less than a year after its creation, thirteen thousand Kodak cameras were sold; most other camera manufacturers counted sales in tens rather than thousands. This enormous success was made possible by Eastman's strategy of producing large quantities of cameras and film cheaply through the use of machinery rather than traditional craft workers. His intention had been to produce a "complete system of practical photography," and in this, he was entirely successful. He had demystified photography and made it available to everyone.

Eastman's forward-thinking philosophy did not please everybody. Die-hard amateurs who liked to develop their own snapshots considered the Kodak an intrusion. Their complaints were hardly heard, however, amid the excitement of the general public.

Reverend Hannibal

For two years, Henry Reichenbach, the research chemist Eastman had hired, struggled to formulate a strong, transparent base for photographic emulsion. Success finally came late in 1888 when he concocted a type of film that was both transparent and strong. A delighted Reichenbach hurried to perfect the manufacturing process so that it could be patented. To his surprise, however, the patent office said that a similar formula had already been presented twelve years earlier by an amateur photographer, a reverend, named Hannibal Goodwin. A legal argument over who had perfected the formula raged intermittently for the next twenty-five years, even as Eastman's company used Reichenbach's process to produce film.

Eastman anticipated that the new film would be a success and would, therefore, replace all others. Consequently, he installed expensive machinery and equipment in his factory to produce the film. This included a perfectly smooth glass table on which the film was prepared and cut into strips. The costly investment proved worthwhile, however. Just two years after its invention, Reichenbach's film was spooled and sold as rolls. This meant that photographers did not have to return their cameras to the Eastman factory to be reloaded with film. They just bought a new roll and loaded it into the Kodak camera themselves. It was not long before Eastman's factory had to struggle to keep up with the demand for the new film.

Big, bigger, biggest

As the Kodak camera became established in the United States, George Eastman explored commercial possibilities in other parts of the world. He saw the whole world as one enormous marketplace. In 1889, the Eastman Photographic Materials Company Limited was established in London, England. It was through this outlet that products manufactured in the United States were distributed to Europe, the Far East, and Australia. Two years later, the worldwide demand for cameras and film had increased so dramatically that a manufacturing factory was built on the outskirts of London. Then, during the 1890s,

Above: Some Kodak advertising encouraged people to use a camera to keep a permanent record of good times.

Opposite page: Testimonials from famous people were part of Eastman's publicity campaign. Robert Peary, the first man to reach the North Pole, was one of those to tell the world how he felt about Eastman's products.

These photographs were taken in the late 1800s. The black-and-white prints were hand tinted by touch-up artists.

Eastman set up a company in Paris called Kodak SAF and one in Berlin called Kodak GMBH.

While the London factory was being constructed, a major change took place at the company's headquarters in Rochester, New York. Tired of the frequent moves to larger premises as his business expanded, Eastman purchased a plot of land outside the city and built a factory complex called Kodak Park. Then, in 1892, realizing that his word *Kodak* had become as recognizable as his own name, George Eastman added it to his company's name. The Eastman Dry Plate and Film Company became the Eastman Kodak Company.

All over the world

During the 1880s, Eastman products had been sold in "sole agency" outlets. These were usually pharmacies owned and run by a single person and specially selected to stock and sell Eastman Kodak products. Each outlet was guaranteed a distribution area in which there were no rivals. This method of sale also meant that Eastman Kodak did not have to spend money to purchase properties and pay staff to run them.

By the early 1890s, however, when Eastman was in his late thirties, he decided that it would be worthwhile for Kodak to have its own distribution outlets. These outlets were owned by Kodak, but they were run and operated as separate companies. All the companies bore the name of Kodak and in doing so, further publicized the company and its products. The outlets sold only Kodak products and catered both to the general public and to other businesses and professionals. It was not long before these Kodak outlets appeared all over the world. By the turn of the twentieth century, there were Kodak outlets in France, Germany, Australia, and Egypt.

Eastman was eager to convey quality at his stores. The last thing he wanted was for his products to be tarnished by the appearance of an untidy showroom. Also, in many Kodak establishments, customers were encouraged to watch a free photography demonstration, a quick show aimed at convincing them that

Above: A British advertisement from the early 1890s emphasized the Kodak's simplicity.

Below: Paints were used to tint daguerreotypes and other early photographic prints.

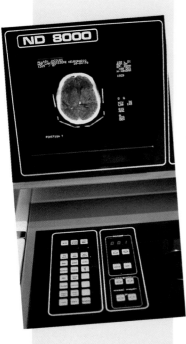

photography was a simple and enjoyable pastime. The strategy worked well, and many people bought cameras before leaving the stores.

New uses for photography

George Eastman wanted the word *Kodak* to be familiar to everyone—from children to royalty. He also wanted Kodak to be associated with only things that were perceived to be good

By the mid-1890s, more than one hundred thousand Kodak cameras had been sold, and 300 miles of film were being manufactured every month. Eastman's determination to achieve his goal of making photography universally popular had succeeded at last.

Most of the photographs taken were of relatives or at family gatherings, but photography was also used in many diverse and less obvious ways. In 1895, for example, a German physicist named

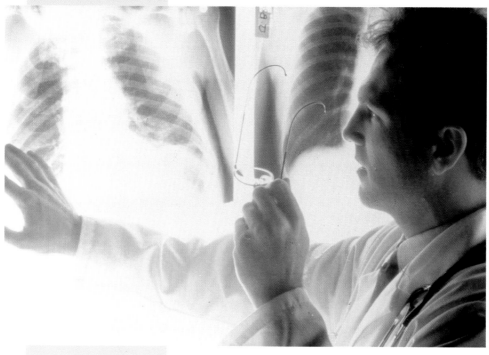

Wilhelm Roentgen discovered X rays. The benefits of X rays were quickly established, and as soon as scientists realized that X rays could be developed as photographs, Eastman became interested. A year later, Kodak began to produce commercially available X-ray plates.

Likewise, during the 1890s, Thomas Edison, the inventor of the lightbulb, had been thinking about making a movie camera. One of the problems that confronted Edison—and others who wanted to make movie cameras—was that most film was inadequate for the endeavor. Movie film had to be strong and transparent, and it was not until Edison discovered Eastman's new film that he found what he needed. Edison produced a "kinetoscope," the forerunner of the modern movie camera. This invention, coupled with the new Eastman film, marked the arrival of the film industry. This new industry ultimately had a huge impact on ordinary people's lives and also created a colossal new market for Eastman's products.

As Thomas Edison and like-minded inventors continued to improve the development of the movie camera, Eastman made sure that Kodak continually marketed improved film. The demand for movie, or "cine," film, as it was known, was so great that Kodak found it difficult to produce enough.

New designs

George Eastman was the driving force behind Kodak, but a man named Frank Brownell also played an important role. Brownell was a camera designer who made cameras for Kodak while also running his own company. Eastman, always a thoughtful employer and kind friend, praised Brownell, saying that he was "The greatest camera designer the world has known."

During his seventeen-year association with Kodak, Brownell made and designed sixty different types of cameras. Among the most important were the Folding Kodak and the Pocket Kodak. Until these two went on the market, most cameras were box

Above: Eastman held his own Kodak box camera as he prepared to take a shot.

Opposite, top: Kodak produced some medical equipment, such as this scanner. By 1981, about one-fifth of Kodak's sales were from items not related to photography.

Opposite, bottom: Kodak began to produce X-ray plates commercially just one year after the discovery of the X ray.

31

Below: During the 1990s, Kodak tried to minimize pollution and save energy at their plants.

shaped and fairly cumbersome. The new cameras folded in half, collapsing like bellows. In addition, their film was contained in cartridges and could, therefore, be loaded and unloaded in daylight. The Folding Pocket Kodak was another best-selling design of Brownell's. It was small enough to be folded up and slipped into a pocket. Just five years later, nearly 1.5 million Kodak cameras had been sold, and film was being produced at the rate of 400 miles per month.

Below: These large complexes are modern-day Kodak factories in England.

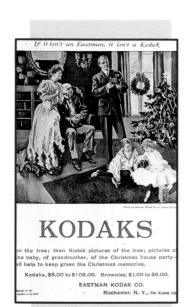

If it isn't an Eastman, it isn't a Kodak

KODAKS

on the tree; then Kodak pictures of the tree; pictures of the baby, *of* grandmother, of the Christmas house party—all help to keep green the Christmas memories.

Kodaks, $5.00 to $108.00. Brownies, $1.00 to $9.00.

EASTMAN KODAK CO.

Rochester, N. Y., *The Kodak City*

With the Brownie camera, Eastman realized his goal of creating a camera that could be sold for just a dollar.

This increasing growth in sales enabled Kodak to continue its expansion. George Eastman took over other companies; he generally bought them outright for lump sums. More often than not, these companies were moved—equipment, personnel, and all—to Kodak Park. Eastman also bought patents so that he had the ownership rights to other companies' products and inventions.

To a slightly nervous Henry Strong, it seemed that the company was growing too fast. Strong feared that sales would start to decline and that the company would collapse. Strong trusted Eastman, however, and was reassured when Eastman told him that the only way forward for Kodak was to reinvest money in the company.

Gaining a monopoly

Strong was not the only person who was concerned. Many people feared that Kodak might be weakened by its speedy growth and believed that there was not enough of a market for all its products. Eastman, however, believed that the best way to succeed was to continually improve and increase the range of products and to keep one step ahead of any competing company. He advised Strong, "If we can get out improved goods every year nobody will be able to follow us and compete with us."

Some people felt that as Kodak became bigger and had less competition in the world of photography, the huge company began to monopolize the business. This meant that Kodak alone set the price of photography equipment. People worried that Kodak would increase its prices and that interested buyers would have no choice but to pay them. Eastman, however, hoped to do the opposite. He wanted to make photography as inexpensive as possible. Specifically, he wanted to manufacture a camera that could be sold for just one dollar.

Shares

In 1898, the British company of Eastman Photographic Materials and the Eastman Kodak Company

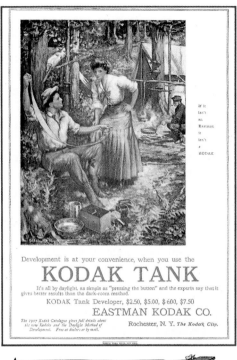

Development is at your convenience, when you use the

KODAK TANK

It's all by daylight, as simple as "pressing the button" and the experts say that it gives better results than the dark-room method.

KODAK Tank Developer, $2.50, $5.00, $600, $7.50

EASTMAN KODAK CO.

The 1907 Kodak Catalogue gives full details about the new Kodaks and the Daylight Method of Development. Free at dealers or by mail.

Rochester, N. Y. *The Kodak City.*

Above left: The Kodak developing tank was one of the company's many photographic inventions.

Above right: Many specialty items, such as this spy camera, were created at the turn of the century.

Left: This camera, designed by a French scientist, was created to photograph movement.

of Rochester, New York, became a single company named simply Kodak Limited. Kodak Limited owned everything Kodak all over the world. This included patents, outlets, factories, and equipment. The new

Above: Kodak's catalog of products (cover of the 1915 catalog pictured) became famous. Kodak sold more than a million copies in a year.

Right: Kodak targeted specific markets for each of its cameras. This advertisement for the Folding Pocket Kodak was intended to interest tourists.

company was based in London, England, the commercial capital of the world at that time, but maintained the production facility at Kodak Park. Kodak Limited also became a public company. This meant that people could buy stock shares and invest in the company. The money from the shares would be used to make the business more profitable.

Shares in Kodak Limited sold out as soon as they became available on the stock market. With the huge influx of money that came from these purchases, Kodak Limited had enormous resources at its disposal, and George Eastman once again looked to the future.

The first "divvy"

As the company grew, Eastman did not spend as much time on experiments with ideas. Instead, he spent much of his time making business decisions. He also frequently walked through the factories and chatted with his employees as he went. He made it obvious to all his workers that they could approach him if they had a problem. He also encouraged his workforce to come up with ideas that might improve efficiency. As an incentive, he offered bonuses for smart suggestions.

A year after he introduced the suggestions system, Eastman made another astounding decision. He

shared with his employees the huge personal profit he had made when Kodak Limited was first put on the stock market. At the time, this was an unprecedented move, but Eastman believed that his employees contributed to the success of Kodak and, therefore, deserved some kind of reward. He had founded the company on mutual respect between employees and employer.

In all, Eastman dispensed $178,000 among about three thousand people in what he called the "divvy." As the company grew, the divvy was formalized into a profit-sharing plan. George Eastman thought it was only fair that the workers and shareholders benefit if the company made a profit at the end of a year.

The Brownie

Soon after the dawn of the twentieth century, camera designer Frank Brownell came up with a design that satisfied all Eastman's requirements. It was named "the Brownie," and within a year, nearly 250,000 had been sold. The Brownie was very simple to use, and this was why it was such a success. The design was so good that it remained much the same for approximately eighty years. Unlike any other camera, the Brownie was made specifically for children, and its sales potential was ruthlessly exploited. Brownie

Above: In the early 1900s, Kodak outlets offered free demonstrations to get people into their shops.

Below: The Brownie, named after camera designer Frank Brownell, was an early Kodak success.

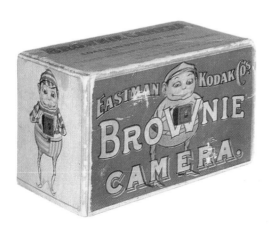

Above: Eastman gave his employees benefits such as profit sharing, a unique business practice for the time.

Below: This French illustration shows filmmakers shooting footage of a battle.

LES DANGERS DU REPORTAGE A LA GUERRE
Deux opérateurs de cinématographe qui l'ont échappé belle

clubs were organized, and photographic competitions were arranged.

Perhaps the most important thing about the Brownie, though, besides its simple and effective design, was its price. It cost just one dollar. Its film cartridge contained six exposures and cost fifteen cents, and it cost only forty-five cents to get prints made. Eastman had achieved his goal of creating an inexpensive camera that anyone could use.

Looking after the work force

In 1904, George Eastman made some company changes that greatly benefited his workers. First, he reduced his employees' working hours from ten to nine hours a day with no loss of pay. He believed that this was something his efficient workers deserved.

Next, Eastman decided to make the factory work environment safe for his workers. Cellulose nitrate, the chemical Kodak originally used as a base for film, was flammable. This had been discovered when a stock of X-ray film caught fire. Concerned about safety, Eastman changed the chemicals used on his film, and in 1908, Kodak started to produce a safety film that was not dangerous. Eastman also created a committee at Kodak whose job it was to look into accident prevention. This was a wise precaution since many of the chemicals and compounds used in the production of film were extremely poisonous. Finally, in 1911, Eastman created an accident, benefit, and pension fund for all his employees, a work force that now numbered more than five thousand.

A private man

George Eastman was a private man. He never married and devoted almost all of his life to his business. His life and character were full of contradictions. He was a tough, competitive businessman, yet he was also capable of extraordinary acts of generosity. He made photography universally popular but was so

To relax, Eastman
enjoyed camping
trips with friends.

unassuming and modest that few photographs were ever taken of him.

It has been said that Eastman had little time for recreation before he was fifty years old. When he did relax, though, he enjoyed tinkering in his workshop or repairing his hunting lodge in North Carolina. He loved to fish, read, and listen to music. He also liked active vacations and went on safari in Africa and on camping expeditions with friends.

Music was a lifelong passion of Eastman's although he had no musical ability himself. He had an organ in his home, and he liked to have someone play for him while he ate his meals. He founded and sponsored the Rochester Symphony Orchestra and the University of Rochester's Eastman School of Music.

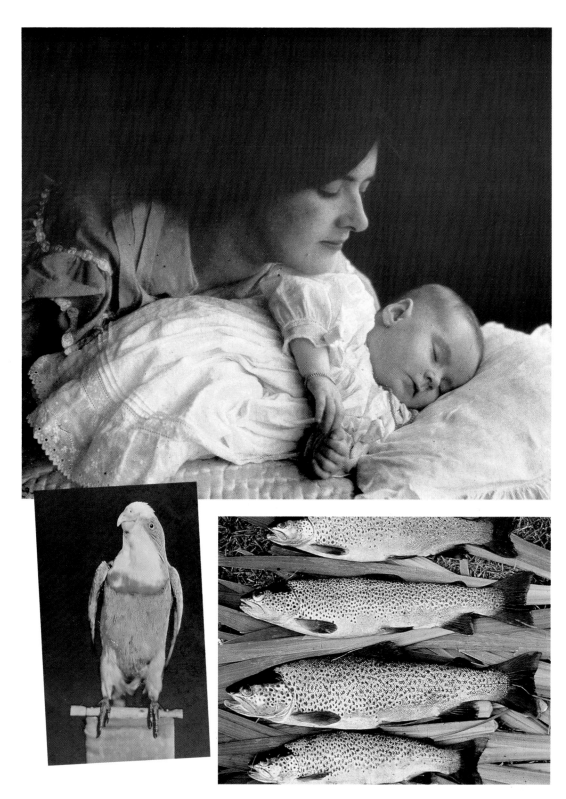

Another of his interests was medicine. Eastman helped establish a school of medicine and a hospital at the University of Rochester. He also founded a dental clinic there. This dental clinic was so popular that similar clinics were set up in London, Paris, Rome, Stockholm, and Brussels. In 1994, the London clinic was still England's foremost dental research and education facility.

Establishing a research laboratory

At the end of 1911, George Eastman took a tour of the chemical factory of a German company called Bayer. It was revealed that the German company employed several hundred research scientists. Eastman did not like to admit that Kodak employed only ten chemists.

Eastman was determined to change the situation. He realized that Kodak would fall behind other companies in developing products if it did not have the right staff to carry out necessary research. Eastman needed to find and hire a scientist who would be able to establish a Kodak research laboratory.

Eventually, Eastman learned of Englishman Dr. Charles Mees, who, although only thirty years old, was joint managing director of a small but successful photographic firm named Wratten and Wainwright. Eastman approached Charles Mees with the offer of a job, and Mees accepted without hesitation. He knew, however, that Wratten and Wainwright would probably stop production if he left. So, Mees told Eastman that, to get Mees's services, Kodak Limited would have to buy Wratten and Wainwright as well. Eastman agreed and bought the entire English company. All of the employees at Wratten and Wainwright were offered similar jobs at Kodak Limited in England. There were no lost jobs, and everybody was happy—most of all, George Eastman.

The following year, in another generous gesture, Eastman gave $1.5 million worth of Kodak stock to the Massachusetts Institute of Technology (MIT), a university that he had always admired and that had

Opposite: The early processes of adding color to photographs progressed from hand-tinting through several stages to the autochrome system (top) created in 1907.

• • • • • • • • • • • • • • • • • •

"What we do in our working hours determines what we have; what we do in our leisure hours determines what we are."

—George Eastman
• • • • • • • • • • • • • • • • • •

supplied a number of skilled Kodak employees. The donation was made in the name of "Smith," and people wondered who the mysterious Mr. Smith really was. "What I desire to avoid as far as possible is the notoriety which oftentimes accompanies such gifts," George Eastman explained. It was only after eight years of speculation that Eastman revealed that he was the donor. By the time of his death, Eastman was believed to have given more than $20 million to MIT.

Mees gets to work

In 1912, Mees moved to the United States and started work on the construction of a research facility at Kodak Park. He brought several trusted colleagues from England with him. Workers in Rochester called it the "English Invasion." At the beginning of 1913, the research building was ready. It was one of the first commercial research laboratories established in the United States.

Eastman encouraged Mees to research whatever he liked. Eastman explained Mees's job description as "Your mission is the future of photography." To some, this might have been intimidating, but Mees considered it the chance he had wanted for years. He did warn Eastman not to expect too much too soon, however, and said that it would probably be about ten years before he and his team came up with anything that would be of any use.

Mees was not entirely right. The scientists soon produced a type of X-ray film that had commercial potential. Also, by 1914, a new film named Kodachrome was developed by John Capstaff. The development of Kodachrome was exciting since it used red and green colors rather than just black and white. The printed results were satisfactory for portraits but were of limited use for other subjects.

Hannibal makes a comeback

Kodak found itself in trouble in 1913 as a result of the dispute over Hannibal Goodwin's film processing patent. This dispute had began back in 1889.

Opposite: Eastman, at age sixty, was still working hard and encouraging new research.

Goodwin had died in 1900, and his firm, the Goodwin Film and Camera Company, was taken over by a large corporation called Ansco. Eastman had tried to resolve the question of who owned Goodwin's patent, but it was a complicated matter. Over the years, various judges had been confused by lawyers and legal arguments about complicated chemical formulas. The matter was finally resolved in 1913 when Kodak was ordered to pay Ansco $5 million for the patent. Eastman was angered by the decision but was glad to be free of the problem. In exchange for the huge sum of money, Kodak was granted the right to use Goodwin's patented product.

More legal disputes followed, though. The U.S. attorney general warned Eastman that the government had concerns about Kodak gaining a monopoly in the photography market; monopolizing any U.S. business market is illegal. The government worried that Kodak was buying up other photography com-

This hand-tinted photograph was used to promote Kodak film and printing-out paper. Eastman liked to use the theme of a happy family in his advertisements, aimed at what he saw as a growing market.

panies so that it could dictate product prices and eliminate competition. George Eastman refuted the allegations, but the attorney general's office filed a lawsuit against Kodak. Two years later, a judge decided that Kodak Limited was, in fact, a monopoly. Eastman immediately appealed the decision, and another saga of legal wrangling began.

The war years

When the United States entered World War I in 1917, the deeply patriotic George Eastman offered his services, and those of his company, to the U.S. government. The War Department was quick to accept Kodak's offer to supply the chemical to waterproof the fragile wings of aircraft, the same chemical used to make film bases. The government was slower to pick up Eastman's idea of aerial photography.

Eventually, the U.S. military recognized that photographs could play an important role in documenting and planning military strategies on the ground. In the spring of 1918, a school of aerial photography opened in Rochester, and by the end of the war in November 1918, more than one million aerial photographs had been taken from planes as they flew over the battlefields of northern France.

Just as the United States entered the war, Kodak also put on the market a camera that was advertised as "The Soldier's Kodak Camera." It had been made specifically for the young men who were destined to cross the Atlantic to fight.

Boom years

World War I actually led to an increase in the popularity of photography. By the time the fighting ended in 1918, people all over the world were familiar with snapshots. Although comparatively few pictures were taken of actual battles, many thousands were taken of loved ones at home and of soldiers leaving for the front. Photographs of political leaders and generals were regularly published in daily newspapers and, in this way, photography became an accepted part of daily life.

During World War I, snapshots became more popular than ever, as loved ones exchanged photographs before being separated by the war.

The Wizard of Oz, *filmed in 1939, reflected the advances in moviemaking technology Kodak and the Technicolor Corporation jointly achieved.*

In 1920, Kodak sold five times as many cameras as it had in 1914, when the war started in Europe. To boost this new enthusiasm for photography, Kodak initiated massive advertising campaigns.

As business boomed, Kodak soon made a significant move. It started a company called the Tennessee Eastman Company whose job it was to manufacture the wood alcohol from which film base was made. This made perfect business sense from Eastman's point of view since it meant that his company no longer needed to buy wood alcohol from another supplier. Within ten years, the Tennessee Eastman Company was producing a range of Kodak products that had little or nothing to do with photography.

The postwar years were also profitable for the movie industry. Moviemaking had come a long way. In 1903, a silent movie entitled *The Great Train*

Robbery was made. It lasted just fifteen minutes, but this was considered such a long time that notices were posted outside theaters where the film was shown to warn potential customers that they might get bored. Twenty years later, however, movies that lasted an hour or more could hardly be produced fast enough to satisfy the demand from the American and European public. Because Kodak supplied most Hollywood moviemakers with film, the industry proved to be a huge source of revenue for the company.

Early in the 1920s, Kodak forged a working relationship with the Technicolor Corporation. Between them, the two companies made significant advances in the lucrative world of moviemaking, and they took out patents on each new innovation they made. This eventually led to a clash with the U.S. government, which accused the two businesses of conspiring to monopolize the movie industry. Despite this confrontation, many years later, Kodak received the ultimate accolade when it was awarded an Academy Award for its contribution to the movie industry.

Home movies

As Hollywood established itself as the place for professional moviemaking, Eastman sensed that there might be a similar market for amateur moviemaking closer to home. After many years of research and experimentation, Kodak released a practical home movie camera in 1923. It was called the Cine-Kodak Motion Picture Camera and came with a projector called the Kodascope. The problem with the new camera was it was very expensive compared with a still camera.

Not surprisingly, sales of the home movie camera were slow at first, but as people started to use cameras to document things other than family get-togethers, sales increased. Operations were filmed in hospitals so that new techniques could be passed on to students. For the first time, films were also used in schools. This led to the creation of a new Kodak company, the Eastman Teaching Films Corporation.

The movie industry enjoyed a golden age after World War I. Kodak benefited from this growth as the company produced the majority of the film used in Hollywood.

The Cine-Kodak Motion Picture Camera still used black-and-white film, but George Eastman wanted to change that. Encouraged by Eastman himself, Kodak researchers came up with Kodacolor film in 1928. To launch this new technology, Eastman held a party at his Rochester home and invited the country's most important leaders and industrialists, including his old friend Thomas Edison, to attend.

On the afternoon of the party, each guest was given the opportunity to use a movie camera loaded with Kodacolor film. The films were developed and shown to the whole gathering in the evening. To Eastman's delight, Kodacolor received universal approval and, as was his way, he used the many complimentary remarks as testimonials to promote the film when it went on sale. One problem with Kodacolor, however, was that it could not be reprinted. Only one edition could be made, so its use was limited to home movies.

A good place to work

One of the most remarkable things about George Eastman was that he never forgot his workforce or took it for granted. He was a tough businessman and hard negotiator, but he always appreciated hard work and went further than the vast majority of employers to help his employees.

He had introduced profit sharing and the Eastman Savings and Loan Association, which encouraged employees to save money. He had given one-third of his Kodak shares to his employees in 1919, and he had made it possible for men and women to take out loans from the Eastman bank so that they could buy their own homes.

An exclusive insurance plan was also initiated. An employee could take out a policy that guaranteed a pension at retirement or a lump sum payment in the event of death or a disabling accident. Few other companies offered such benefits. In return, Eastman expected—and got—loyalty and

commitment from his work force.

New roles

In 1923, when George Eastman was sixty-nine years old, he relinquished responsibility for the operations of Kodak Limited and became chairman of the board of directors. It became his duty to hear his fellow directors' ideas and to put decisions into practice. He fully intended to give Kodak and its management room to develop without his domineering presence.

Eager to remain active, he headed off on a safari in 1926 to collect specimens for the American Museum of Natural History. He enjoyed the safari so much that he repeated his trip the following year at the age of seventy-three.

Eastman kept himself occupied with other personal interests as well, but as he aged, he became increasingly inactive. He began to suffer from arteriosclerosis, or hardening of the arteries. He found

Above: Eastman, pictured here in his home library, enjoyed reading as well as more active pastimes.

Opposite top: Eastman and his friend inventor Thomas Edison (right) were caught on film—while filming. Edison was one of the influential people who attended the 1928 launch party for Kodacolor film.

Opposite bottom: A 1932 advertisement shows the ease of traveling with a Kodak.

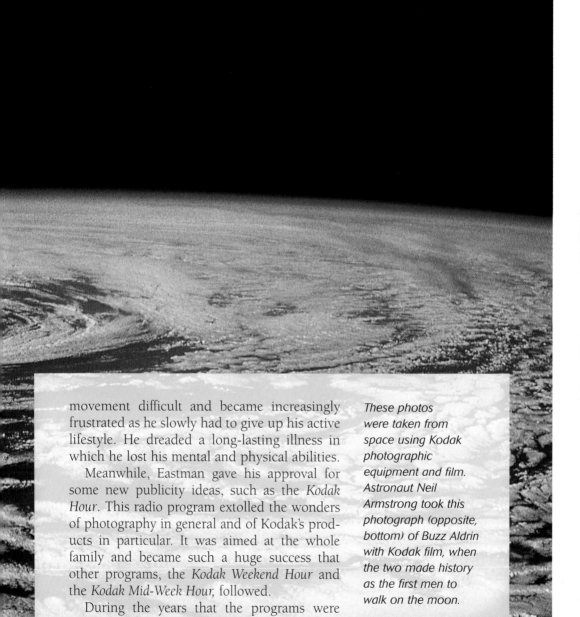

movement difficult and became increasingly frustrated as he slowly had to give up his active lifestyle. He dreaded a long-lasting illness in which he lost his mental and physical abilities.

Meanwhile, Eastman gave his approval for some new publicity ideas, such as the *Kodak Hour*. This radio program extolled the wonders of photography in general and of Kodak's products in particular. It was aimed at the whole family and became such a huge success that other programs, the *Kodak Weekend Hour* and the *Kodak Mid-Week Hour,* followed.

During the years that the programs were broadcast, Kodak produced a range of inexpensive

These photos were taken from space using Kodak photographic equipment and film. Astronaut Neil Armstrong took this photograph (opposite, bottom) of Buzz Aldrin with Kodak film, when the two made history as the first men to walk on the moon.

cameras to suit different age groups. There were cameras for teenagers, fashionable ones for fashionable adults, and even a plastic one called the Baby Brownie.

Compassion

For many years, George Eastman had been an immensely wealthy man, but he saw little reason to hoard his money. He preferred to put it to good use, and during the last half of his life, he gave away the bulk of his fortune. In particular, Eastman wanted better opportunities to be available for African Americans. This led him to sponsor the Hampton and Tuskegee Institutes, which educated black people in teaching and community work.

On occasion, Eastman's generosity started adverse speculation and publicity. After a particularly generous round of donations in 1923, many people began to believe that he was about to retire. In response, he issued a reassuring statement to his staff that also gave an account of his donations. He had given $4.5 million to MIT, $3 million to the University of Rochester's Eastman School of Music, $2.5 million to its College of Arts and Sciences, $1.5 million to its School of Medicine, $1.5 million to its College for Women, and $1 million each to the Hampton and Tuskegee Institutes.

By the 1930s, Eastman had retired from Kodak Limited. He was still very interested in its affairs, but he left the routine managerial decisions to others. His health had continued to decline, and on March 14, 1932, he invited some friends to his home to witness an amendment to his will that would give most of his remaining wealth to the University of Rochester. After he signed the document, Eastman went upstairs and shot himself. He left a note that said, "My work is done. Why wait?" He ended his life in the same controlled, orderly way in which he had lived it.

George Eastman had managed to be both a successful inventor and a successful businessman, a rare combination. There is hardly a place in the world where his famous company is not known.

Progress

Eastman died at a time of change within the photographic world. The days of hit-or-miss experimentation to discover new emulsions and formulas were over. New cameras and different types of film were now the products of intense scientific research.

The scope of research that took place at the Rochester and other Kodak laboratories became increasingly diverse. Cameras, film bases, and chemicals were all studied, and this led to other discoveries. As more research was carried out, more viable products were invented and ultimately manufactured, if not by Kodak Limited, then by one of its increasing number of subsidiary companies. One of these companies produced and researched gelatin, for example, and the Tennessee Eastman Company

53

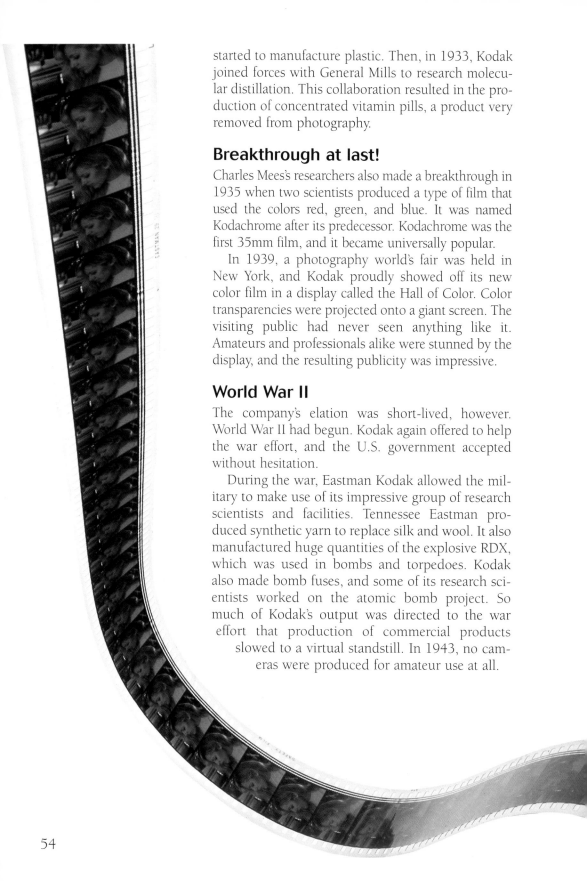

started to manufacture plastic. Then, in 1933, Kodak joined forces with General Mills to research molecular distillation. This collaboration resulted in the production of concentrated vitamin pills, a product very removed from photography.

Breakthrough at last!

Charles Mees's researchers also made a breakthrough in 1935 when two scientists produced a type of film that used the colors red, green, and blue. It was named Kodachrome after its predecessor. Kodachrome was the first 35mm film, and it became universally popular.

In 1939, a photography world's fair was held in New York, and Kodak proudly showed off its new color film in a display called the Hall of Color. Color transparencies were projected onto a giant screen. The visiting public had never seen anything like it. Amateurs and professionals alike were stunned by the display, and the resulting publicity was impressive.

World War II

The company's elation was short-lived, however. World War II had begun. Kodak again offered to help the war effort, and the U.S. government accepted without hesitation.

During the war, Eastman Kodak allowed the military to make use of its impressive group of research scientists and facilities. Tennessee Eastman produced synthetic yarn to replace silk and wool. It also manufactured huge quantities of the explosive RDX, which was used in bombs and torpedoes. Kodak also made bomb fuses, and some of its research scientists worked on the atomic bomb project. So much of Kodak's output was directed to the war effort that production of commercial products slowed to a virtual standstill. In 1943, no cameras were produced for amateur use at all.

When the fighting ended in 1945, the public, which had not been able to take photographs for so long resumed taking pictures with passion. Kodak quickly resupplied the market with new products and invested heavily in updates for its equipment. In 1949, a new Kodacolor film was launched. It was surprisingly slow to take off, however. Determined to help the film sell, Kodak started an advertising campaign and took every opportunity it could to promote its products.

In 1950, Kodak employed a new strategy to advertise its name and products. That year, the company was hired to decorate the main terminal of New York City's

Above: Though these cameras may be Japanese or German, inside them is probably Kodak film, a product used worldwide.

Opposite: This strip of Kodak film represents just one of the many advancements Eastman's company made in the industry of photography.

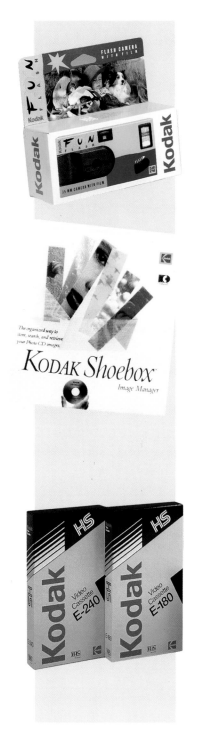

Grand Central Station. The result was the first of many eighteen-by-sixty-foot color transparencies called a "Colorama." These enormous pictures were actually negatives projected onto a huge screen. The Coloramas were viewed by 650,000 people every day. Magazines and newspapers often featured stories on the Colorama. Every time this happened, Kodak received free publicity. The Colorama remained in place until 1989 when Grand Central Station was renovated.

In 1951, Eastman Kodak set up more research facilities in the United States. It also added new ones in England, France, and Australia.

Instamatics and Polaroids

In the mid-1960s, Kodak Limited employed more than one hundred thousand people all over the world, and worldwide sales topped $2 billion for the first time. Japanese and German 35mm cameras, however, had begun to offer Kodak legitimate competition. So, Kodak developed a new type of camera, the Instamatic. It echoed the essential designs of the first Brownie.

Instamatics came in various grades of sophistication. The most expensive had built-in flash units and light meters. All were compact, simple to use, and reliable. Film came in a plastic cartridge and was very easy to load and unload. Even the camera's name suited the heady days of the 1960s. Kodak sold more than 70 million Instamatics. The Pocket Instamatic resulted in an additional 25 million sales.

In 1976, Kodak got involved in the lucrative market of instant photography. The company manufactured cameras and a special film that developed snapshots into prints soon after exposure. Unfortunately for Kodak, a company named Polaroid had already produced similar cameras and film and had taken out patents on various designs. Legal advisers assured Kodak that its products did not interfere with the Polaroid patents and that there was therefore no reason for concern.

As soon as the Kodak instant cameras were released on the market, however, Polaroid sued

Kodak, claiming that some patents had been copied. After a legal battle that lasted ten years, the courts supported Polaroid in its case. Kodak immediately recalled all its instant cameras and compensated their owners. In 1991, Kodak was ordered to pay Polaroid $924.5 million.

The wisdom of varied products

In an effort to find a new product to take over where the Instamatic left off, Kodak began to produce disk cameras in 1982. Instead of rolled film, these small cameras used tiny negatives held on a computer disk. The design and engineering of the system was brilliant, but the concept was flawed. In all, around 25 million disk cameras were sold before production was halted in 1988. To Kodak, this was almost a failure; the company had hoped that the disk system would be its most successful yet. The competition, mainly from Japanese companies, stayed with 35mm cameras and, for the first time, Kodak was not a market leader.

Although Kodak struggled with the disk camera during the 1980s, the company still consistently made profits. One reason for this was its interests in profitable industries other than photography. During the 1950s, Tennessee Eastman had manufactured artificial thread for rugs and curtains, and Texas Eastman synthesized chemicals from oil and gas. In the 1960s Carolina Eastman produced Kodel polyester for making clothes. Ten years later, the Arkansas Eastman Company had made organic chemicals.

By 1980, the year of Kodak's one-hundredth anniversary, the company had begun to produce a blood analyzer. In 1981, Kodak sales exceeded $10 billion, nearly 20 percent of which came from products unrelated to photography.

In the 1990s, Kodak manufactured laser printers, home improvement materials, photocopiers, and videotapes. The company maintained its research departments as well. In 1993 alone, Kodak was granted 1,008 patents in the United States.

Opposite and above: By the 1990s, Kodak manufactured a wide variety of products, many of which had little or nothing to do with photography.

The future

In spite of all these different interests, Kodak will always be linked with photography, and the company has remained dedicated to research new photographic products. During the 1990s, Kodak explored and developed a completely new photographic system, the Photo CD. With this system, images are transferred onto a compact disc, from which they can be relayed

Due to the versatility of modern film, important events around the world can be captured clearly. The 1988 Olympic games in Seoul (main photo), the fall of the Berlin Wall (top), and an oil well fire in the Middle East, (below) were all such noteworthy events.

In 1990, Kodak launched
its Photo CD system
(pictured).

onto a television screen or transmitted through a telephone line. It is a system that uses the innovative technology that Kodak continually researches in an effort to stay ahead of the competition.

By the mid-1990s, Kodak marketed two thousand Kodak products in more than 150 countries. It still adhered, however, to many of George Eastman's ideals and concepts. One of these was a concern for the environment. Kodak recycled products whenever possible. In keeping with this philosophy in 1990, it had introduced a family of fun cameras for single use only. These inexpensive cameras were sold complete with film, and when the film had been exposed, the camera was returned to a photofinisher. The photofinisher then developed the film and returned the camera case to Kodak, where it was recycled to make a new camera. It was a simple idea that became a huge success. In 1993, more than 100 million single-use cameras were sold, giving Kodak yet another edge in the photography market.

• •

"George Eastman's lively and inventive mind, his gift for organization and management, and his instinctive feel for what the public wanted are still qualities fundamental to Kodak today."

—From *Kodak in the U.K.*,
a Kodak publication

• •

Timeline

1854   July 12: George Eastman is born to George Washington and Maria Kilbourn Eastman, in Waterville, New York.

1868   George Eastman leaves school at the age of fourteen to take a job as a messenger boy for an insurance firm.

1874   Eastman takes a job as a junior clerk at the Rochester Savings Bank, where he earns eight hundred dollars a year.

1878   Eastman becomes interested in wet-plate photography.

1879   Eastman continues to work on perfecting an emulsion recipe for use with photographic dry plates. Later in the year, he produces and patents a machine that coats plates with emulsion and makes mass-production possible.

1880   April: Eastman goes into business manufacturing dry plates in Rochester, New York.

1881   Henry Strong forms a partnership with Eastman, and the Eastman Dry Plate Company is formed.
September: With the growing success of his new company, Eastman leaves his job at the bank to devote more time to his new business.

1882   The Eastman Dry Plate Company experiences a problem with the gelatin on the plates and replaces all the faulty merchandise, which gives the company a reputation for quality and fairness.

1884   The Eastman Dry Plate and Film Company is created. Eastman negative paper is introduced but not released for sale until the following year.

1885   Eastman and camera maker William Walker invent the first roll holder for negative paper. Transparent American film is produced.

1888   June: Eastman names his new compact camera "Kodak." It is promoted with the catchphrase, "You push the button—We do the rest."

1889   The Eastman Photographic Materials Company Limited is established in London, England.
August: The first commercial celluloid film is developed and marketed.

1891   Kodak Park is created in Rochester, New York, and a factory is built near London, England. Thomas Edison invents the kinetoscope—the forerunner of the modern movie camera—which heralds the arrival of the movie industry and a whole new market for film.

1892   When he realizes that the name Kodak is at least as famous as his own, Eastman changes the company name to the Eastman Kodak Company.

1895   German physicist Wilhelm Roentgen discovers X rays, which creates another market for Eastman and Kodak. Frank Brownell develops the successful Folding Kodak and Pocket Kodak cameras.

1898   Eastman Photographic Materials in Great Britain and the Eastman Kodak Company of New York are joined into a single company, Kodak Limited.

1899   Eastman begins a profit-sharing scheme among his work force, which becomes known as the divvy.

1900   Frank Brownell develops the hugely successful camera known as the Brownie, which is sold for just one dollar.

1904   Eastman cuts his employees' working day from ten to nine hours, with no pay cut.

1912   The divvy, or wage dividend, is formalized into a profit-sharing scheme.

1913	Kodak's first commercial research laboratory, one of the first laboratories of its kind in the United States, is opened. Kodak faces legal battles over the patent of celluloid film.
1914	Kodak scientist John Capstaff develops a film named Kodachrome, which uses red and green.
1917	The first Eastman dental clinic is established in Rochester; in the years that follow, more such clinics are created in cities all over the world.
1921	U.S. courts rule that Kodak may not buy any companies in the future, to prevent the company from becoming a monopoly.
1923	Kodak releases the home movie camera, the Cine-Kodak Motion Picture Camera. Eastman hands over daily operations of the company to become chairman of the board of directors.
1928	Kodacolor film is first produced. Kodak enters education with the Eastman Teaching Films Corporation.
1930	The company Tennessee Eastman is founded. It eventually manufactures synthetic textiles—the first Kodak products not directly related to photography.
1932	March 14: George Eastman, at age seventy-seven, commits suicide at home after a long illness. He leaves his estate to the University of Rochester.
1935	Kodachrome—a film that uses red, green, and blue—is developed and sold commercially for the first time.
1949	Kodacolor film is finally released on the market.
1950	Kodak wins an Oscar for its production of a safety film to replace the highly flammable cellulose nitrate film that was commonly used in the movie industry.
1963	The hugely popular Kodak Instamatic cameras are introduced—more than 70 million are sold.
1976	Kodak enters the instant camera market and soon runs into trouble with a rival company, Polaroid, which claims that it already owns the patent on the instant camera design.
1991	Kodak is ordered to pay Polaroid $924.5 million to settle the patent battle.
1994	Kodak is ranked as one of the twenty-five largest U.S. companies, with manufacturing facilities on five continents and commercial outlets in more than 150 countries.

Glossary

capital: Assets that a company can invest to make money.

cine camera: A camera that takes a series of still pictures—twenty-four photographs each second—which are then projected onto a screen one after another to give the impression of movement.

company: A group of two or more people that is registered to carry out a trade or business. A company is obliged to conform to certain regulations that may vary from country to country or from state to state in the United States.

company treasurer: An official in a company who is responsible for all the financial matters relating to the company.

copyright: The exclusive right given by law to an inventor or writer to protect his or her invention or work from being copied for a certain period of time.

developing: A process in photography in which a film or plate is treated with chemicals to produce a visible image.

dividend: In business, the sum of money paid out of the company profits to company shareholders. It is usually paid once or twice a year.

entrepreneur: A person who sets up a new business and takes risks in an attempt to make the business successful and profitable.

exposure: The number of individual pictures on a roll of film or the time a piece of film needs to be exposed to the light in order to allow the image to form on the film properly.

film or film base: A strong, flexible, and thin transparent strip that has been coated with photographic emulsion.

gelatin: A natural substance obtained from bone and skin and other animal tissue. It is transparent, has no smell, and is used in the photographic process.

general manager: A person who is elected to organize and lead a company. He or she is responsible for critical decisions that will help the company achieve its business goals.

incorporated or public limited company: A company formed by several owners. Each owner is responsible, by law, for only a limited amount of the company's debts.

invest: To buy shares in a company in the hope that they will make a profit; or to buy an object, such as a house, that will increase in value and therefore make the buyer a profit when the object is eventually sold.

market: In terms of a company's sales plan, the number of people who might want to buy a particular product; it also means to sell the product in an organized and preplanned way.

monopoly: The domination of one company over the sales of a particular product or service, or one particular market, to the extent that it is difficult for other companies to compete. This can mean that the dominant company is able to set its own price level and keep the price unreasonably high because it is the only business that provides the product or service. There are laws against this type of monopoly.

negative: The name given to the image formed on the photographic film after exposure and when the film has been developed. The tones of the image are reversed, with light areas appearing dark and dark areas appearing light.

patent: The legal right granted to an inventor to exclusively make, use, and sell his or her invention for a limited time. To qualify for a patent, the invention must be new and original.

photographic emulsion: A light-sensitive layer with which photographic film is coated.

positive: A positive print is made from a negative image, with the light areas returning to light and dark areas returning to dark.

profit: The amount of money a company or individual has left over in a business venture after costs and expenses have been paid.

share: An equal part of a company's capital that can be bought and owned by a member of the company or the public. If a person buys a share, he or she is then entitled to a percentage of the company's profits.

spool: A reel around which something, such as photographic film, can be wound.

stock market: The place where shares in different companies are bought and sold.

transparency: An individual image on transparent film.

Index